NEW YORK
KNICKS

by Andy Knobel

Published by ABDO Publishing Company, 8000 West 78th Street, Edina, Minnesota 55439. Copyright © 2012 by Abdo Consulting Group, Inc. International copyrights reserved in all countries. No part of this book may be reproduced in any form without written permission from the publisher. SportsZone™ is a trademark and logo of ABDO Publishing Company.

Printed in the United States of America,
North Mankato, Minnesota
062011
092011

 THIS BOOK CONTAINS AT LEAST 10% RECYCLED MATERIALS.

Editor: Dave McMahon
Copy Editor: Anna Comstock
Series design: Christa Schneider
Cover production: Craig Hinton
Interior production: Carol Castro

Photo Credits: Kathy Willens/AP Images, cover; Ron Frehm/AP Images, 1, 7, 25, 33, 43 (middle); AP Images, 4, 12, 18, 21, 29, 42 (top); Dave Pickoff/AP Images, 8, 11, 42 (bottom); John Lent/AP Images, 15; Marty Lederhandler/AP Images, 17, 42 (middle); Focus on Sport/Getty Images, 22; Kathy Willens/AP Images, 26, 43 (top); Bill Kostroun/AP Images, 30; Mark Lennihan/AP Images, 34, 38; Michael Conroy/AP Images, 37; Frank Franklin II/AP Images, 41, 43 (bottom); Stephan Savoia/AP Images, 44; Marty Lederhandler/AP Images, 47

Library of Congress Cataloging-in-Publication Data
Knobel, Andy, 1959-
  New York Knicks / by Andy Knobel.
    p. cm. -- (Inside the NBA500 Includes index.)
  ISBN 978-1-61783-168-3
  1. New York Knickerbockers (Basketball team)--History--Juvenile literature. I. Title.
  GV885.52.N4K66 2012
  796.323'64097471--dc23
                        2011020551

TABLE OF CONTENTS

CHAPTER 1

CAPTAIN AND CLYDE

It was moments before Game 7 of the 1970 National Basketball Association (NBA) Finals. All eyes at Madison Square Garden—the New York Knicks' home arena—were on the tunnel that led from the Knicks' locker room to the court.

Willis Reed's Knicks teammates and their opponents, the Los Angeles Lakers, were wondering anxiously whether Reed would be able to play. The Knicks' center was the NBA regular-season and All-Star Game Most Valuable Player (MVP), but he had a painfully injured upper right leg.

Reed had led New York to the brink of its first championship. But in Game 5, he crumpled to the court with a severely pulled thigh muscle. Without his physical defense in Game 6, Lakers center Wilt Chamberlain had 45 points and 27 rebounds in a 22-point victory. The Knicks' hopes

Willis Reed played only a few minutes in the New York Knicks' Game 7 victory over the Los Angeles Lakers in the 1970 NBA Finals. A leg injury from Game 5 knocked him out of the game, but he inspired his teammates.

seemingly rested on the health of their captain. Doctors and trainers had been treating him.

Suddenly, Reed hobbled into view. He gingerly started warming up. "I hear the roar of the crowd. I see the ovation. I'm saying to myself, 'This is [quite a] predicament,'" Reed recalled. "Because here I am. I'm going to try to play the greatest offensive center in the history of the game—a guy who just got through getting 45 on us—on one leg. And the crowd is yelling, 'Hey, everything's all right, the captain is here!'"

Reed was worried. But Knicks star guard Walt "Clyde" Frazier felt optimistic. "I'll never forget. I saw [Lakers guard Jerry] West, I saw [Lakers forward Elgin] Baylor, I saw Chamberlain stop. They were like mesmerized in watching Willis," Frazier said. "When I saw that, when they stopped warming up, something told me we might have these guys."

Frazier was right. On the Knicks' first possession he fed the ball to Reed. The center hit a shot from behind the foul line for a 2–0 lead. Minutes later, Reed trailed the play, dragging his stiff leg. He took a pass from Dick Barnett and hit a 20-footer from the right wing for

The Knicks' Dave DeBusschere, *left*, and the Los Angeles Lakers' Elgin Baylor collide in Game 1 of the 1970 NBA Finals.

a 5–2 lead. Those were the only points he scored in 27 minutes of play. But his courage inspired the Knicks, demoralized the Lakers, and sent the fans into a frenzy.

"People always talk about [how] last shots win games," Reed said, "but I think the first shot won a game."

The Knicks led 69–42 at halftime. They cruised to a 113–99 win to claim the championship. Frazier had one of the best Game 7 performances in NBA history. He racked up 36 points, 19 assists, seven rebounds, and five steals.

The victory completed a charmed season in which the

Walt Frazier (10), shown keeping the ball from the Lakers' John Egan in May 1970, scored 36 points and made 19 assists in Game 7 of the 1970 NBA Finals.

city of New York seemed destined for glory. In January 1969, the New York Jets of the American Football League (AFL) pulled off an upset to win the first Super Bowl by an AFL team against a team from the National Football League. In October 1969, Major League Baseball's previously hapless New York Mets won their first World Series. "The city was really in a euphoric state," writer Phil Pepe said. "Now it looked like the Knicks were going to do the same thing."

The Knicks had finished the previous regular season by winning 38 of their final 49 games. The team had then reached the Eastern Division finals before falling to the Boston Celtics. The Knicks started the 1969–70 campaign even hotter. Using defense and unselfish ball movement, they won 23 of their first 24 games. This included a then-league-record 18 straight victories.

The last victory in the 18-game winning streak was dramatic. New York fell behind the Cincinnati Royals by five points with 26 seconds remaining. But Reed made two free throws with 16 seconds left. Dave DeBusschere, the Knicks' forward, then stole a pass from Bob Cousy and dunked with six seconds to go. With New York down by one, Reed knocked the ball out of the hands of the Royals' Tom Van Arsdale and into Frazier's. Frazier launched a floater that missed. But he grabbed the rebound and was fouled while shooting with two

"Clyde"

Teammate Dave Stallworth once said of Walt Frazier, "That man is so fast that he could steal the hubcaps off a moving car." Frazier's specialty was chalking up steals, and the 6-foot-4 guard was named to the NBA's All-Defensive first team seven times. He was called "Clyde" because his wide-brimmed hats and flashy suits reminded people of another thief, bank robber Clyde Barrow. Frazier averaged 18.9 points, 6.1 assists, and 5.9 rebounds per game, and he made the Hall of Fame in 1987.

seconds on the clock. He made both free throws for the win.

Then the Knicks cooled off. They went 37–21 the rest of the way. This was good enough for a league-best 60–22 record, but flawed enough to raise doubts. In the first round of the playoffs, New York struggled against the Baltimore Bullets before winning 127–114 in Game 7. Barnett and DeBusschere scored 28 points

"HIT THE OPEN MAN"

Red Holzman's coaching approach was as straightforward as his wardrobe: nine conservative suits of the same style and color.

On defense, the Knicks' coach preached, "See the ball," meaning players should be aware of where the basketball was so they could guard the passing lanes and help out teammates. On offense, it was "Hit the open man," meaning move without the ball and pass it around to create a high-percentage shot.

"Red was a handler of men, a real psychologist," center/forward Jerry Lucas said. "He understood people—he was the ideal coach for this team."

Holzman's methods resulted in 613 victories in two stints as New York's coach—from 1967 to 1977, and then again from 1978 to 1982. Holzman led New York to two NBA titles, and he was elected to the Hall of Fame in 1985.

apiece in that game. New York had an easier time in the Eastern Division finals. The Knicks defeated Lew Alcindor and the Milwaukee Bucks four games to one. Ahead lay the dangerous Lakers in the NBA Finals.

The host Knicks won Game 1 behind 37 points from Reed. They then lost the second game at Madison Square Garden when Chamberlain blocked Reed's last-second shot. The Lakers tied Game 3 on a 60-foot heave by West at the regulation buzzer. But the visiting Knicks sealed the win in overtime on a jumper by Barnett in the final seconds. Again, however, the host Lakers evened the series in Game 4, this time behind 37 points by West.

Game 5 in New York proved crucial. The Lakers led 25–15 with 3 minutes and

Coach Red Holzman led the Knicks to NBA titles in 1970 and 1973.

56 seconds left in the opening quarter when Reed drove on Chamberlain and collapsed in agony. He was lost for the game and seemingly the series. Against all odds, the Knicks rallied without their captain. Using a rare 1–3–1 offensive formation suggested by forward Bill Bradley, New York drew Chamberlain away from the basket. The Knicks prevailed 107–100. Celtics great John Havlicek called it "the greatest comeback in basketball."

New York lost Game 6 without Finals MVP Reed. This set the stage for the Game 7 heroics, which Frazier summarized perfectly. "Willis [Reed] provided the inspiration," he said, "and in a way I provided the devastation."

THE CITY GAME

In New York City, most schools lack the grass fields needed for baseball and football. But nearly every schoolyard has an asphalt court surrounded by a chain-link fence.

And all day and into the night, the *thump, thump, thump* of dribbled basketballs and the *thwack* and *clank* of shots hitting metal backboards and rims provide a soundtrack for the city.

"I never saw a dirt field. Everything was cement," said Nat Militzok, a forward on the first Knicks team in 1946–47. Militzok played high school and college ball in the city. "We had two choices: either go in the schoolyard and play ball or hang around on the corner and get in trouble. So, we played basketball all our lives."

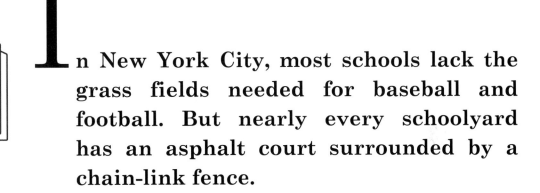

Knicks guard Harry Gallatin grabs a rebound against the Baltimore Bullets during the 1949 BAA Eastern Division semifinals in Baltimore.

Basketball became a big spectator sport in the 1930s. Sportswriter Ned Irish came up with the idea of hosting college doubleheaders at the old Madison Square Garden at the corner of Eighth Avenue and Forty-ninth Street in New York City. Eventually, arena owners in other big cities saw basketball as a way to fill seats. The owners formed a professional league called the Basketball Association of America (BAA) in 1946. The BAA later merged with another league, the National Basketball League (NBL),

creating the NBA. The New York Knicks, owned by Irish, were a part of the BAA. The Knicks played in the league's first game. They defeated the host Toronto Huskies 68–66 on November 1, 1946.

New York hired St. John's University coach Joe Lapchick for its second season, and it became a consistent winner. But the pro game was largely ignored. That changed in the spring of 1951, though, when betting scandals rocked college basketball, including four New York schools. Fans seeking an honest game turned to the NBA, which began play in 1949. The Knicks quickly drew attention by playing in three straight NBA Finals, beginning in 1951.

New York lost the first three games of the best-of-seven 1951 Finals to the Rochester Royals. But the Knicks rallied

Knick Name

Knicks is short for Knickerbockers—a term that traces its origins to the Dutch settlers who came to what is modern-day New York in the 1600s. Father Knickerbocker, who wore a cotton wig, a three-cornered hat, and rolled-up "knickered" pants, became a popular symbol in the late nineteenth and early twentieth centuries.

Representatives of the NBL and BAA gather after agreeing to a merger of the leagues in 1949. Knicks owner Ned Irish, *second from right*, helped to form the new league, the NBA.

with three straight wins to force a Game 7. The visiting Knicks led in the final minutes but could not hold on and lost 79–75. The following season, they met the Minneapolis Lakers in the Finals. Early in the opener, the game officials failed to see and count a clear basket by New York's Al McGuire. The Knicks lost the game in overtime and the series in seven games. New York was denied in the Finals for a third time in 1953. This time, the Knicks lost to the Lakers four games to one.

The Knicks had winning seasons in 11 of their first 13 years. But starting in 1959–60, New York finished last in the

"DOLLAR BILL"

Bill Bradley graduated from Princeton University in 1965 as a three-time basketball All-American. He then enrolled as a Rhodes Scholar at Oxford University in England to pursue his intellectual interests. He thought his basketball career was over.

But after two years away from the sport, he felt he owed it to himself to "test myself against the best." It was a good move. Bradley signed with the Knicks in 1967 for a then-NBA record $500,000 over four years. A selfless passer and accurate shooter, the 6-foot-5 Bradley averaged 12.4 points per game in 10 seasons, mostly as a small forward. He was nicknamed "Dollar Bill" because of his simple, low-cost lifestyle off the court.

Bradley was inducted into the Hall of Fame in 1983 and was a US senator from New Jersey from 1979 to 1997. He ran for president in the Democratic primaries in 2000.

Eastern Division seven consecutive times. The team reached its lowest point on March 2, 1962, when it gave up an NBA-record 100 points to Philadelphia Warriors center Wilt Chamberlain in a 169–147 defeat. By the end of the decade, however, the Knicks would get back at the big man. The turning point came in 1964. That year, New York drafted center/forward Willis Reed. A year later, the Knicks traded for guard Dick Barnett and drafted swingman Bill Bradley. And guard Walt Frazier was added in the 1967 NBA Draft.

Relocated to the new Garden on 8th Avenue and 33rd Street, the Knicks finished 43–39 in 1967–68. They took the defending-champion Philadelphia 76ers to six games before falling in the first round of the playoffs.

The Knicks' Bill Bradley, *right*, tangles with Jeff Mullins of the San Francisco Warriors in 1968.

But New York started the 1968–69 season just 6–13. The club needed a bold move. The Knicks traded four-time All-Star center Walt Bellamy and guard Howard Komives to the Detroit Pistons for forward Dave DeBusschere. The deal let Reed move from forward to center and cleared the point guard spot for Frazier.

The Knicks rallied to finish with a club-record 54 wins. They then swept the Baltimore Bullets in the first round of the playoffs. The Bullets were the league's best regular-season team. New York went on to lose to the defending champion Boston Celtics in six games in the Eastern Division finals. But the future looked bright.

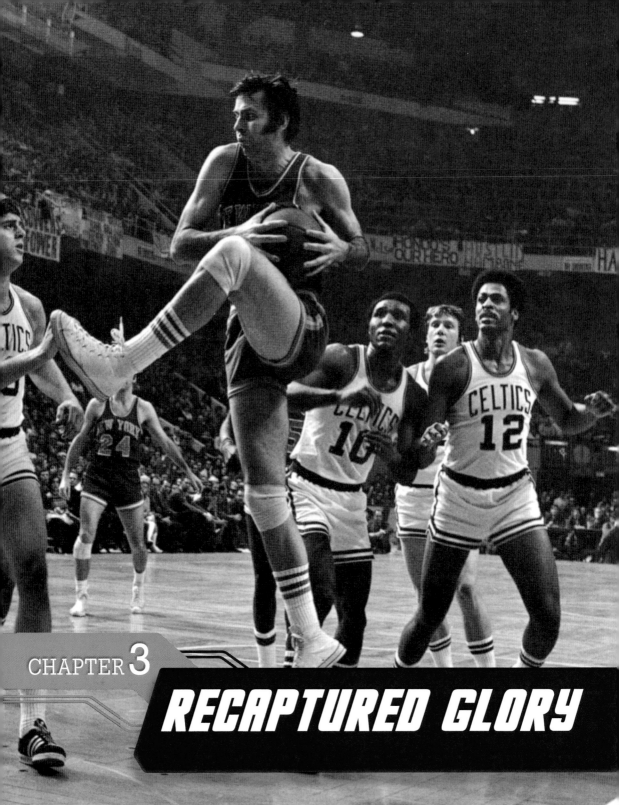

CHAPTER 3

RECAPTURED GLORY

For years, public address announcer John Condon greeted fans entering the Knicks' home arena. He would say, "Good evening, ladies and gentlemen, and welcome to the magical world of Madison Square Garden." And on no night was the Garden more magical than on November 18, 1972.

New York went into that game against the Milwaukee Bucks with a 15–3 record. But the Knicks played most of the contest as if their record were 3–15. Future Hall of Famers Kareem Abdul-Jabbar and Oscar Robertson led Milwaukee. The Bucks were up 86–68 with more than five minutes remaining in the fourth quarter. Then the unthinkable happened. The Knicks chipped away at the lead and eventually won 87–86 by scoring the last 19 points of the game.

Knicks forward Jerry Lucas controls the ball in the 1972 playoffs. He was known for both his defensive play and shooting ability.

Guard Earl "The Pearl" Monroe scored 11 of those 19 points.

"We had a feeling at that time, well, we're destined to do it again," New York forward Dave DeBusschere said. He was alluding to a second world championship. "When we ran off those 19 straight points, we really felt like we couldn't be stopped."

After winning their first championship in 1969–70, the Knicks were stopped the next year in the Eastern Conference finals. They lost Game 7 to the Baltimore Bullets. For the 1971–72 season, New York added two future Hall of Famers in Monroe and Jerry Lucas, a center/forward. The Knicks reached the NBA Finals. But without Willis Reed, who missed nearly the entire season with an injured left knee, the Knicks lost in five games to the Los Angeles Lakers.

In 1973, Reed returned. This gave the veteran Knicks team hope that it could make one more title run. New York struggled with injuries during the regular season and finished with a 57–25 mark. This was the fourth-best record in the NBA. But it was 11 games behind the division-winning Boston Celtics. The Knicks eliminated the Bullets in the first round. New York then had to take on Boston. The Knicks appeared to be

Earl "The Pearl" Monroe grabs a loose ball in front of the Los Angeles Lakers' Jim McMillian at Madison Square Garden in the 1973 NBA Finals.

in control of the series. They went up three games to one with a 117–110 double-overtime win behind 37 points from Walt Frazier. But the Celtics took the next two games. This set up a Game 7 at Boston Garden. Boston had never lost a Game 7 at home during its storied history.

"The consensus was that it was all over for us," Knicks backup guard Dean Meminger said. He made sure it was not so. Meminger was brought in as a defensive replacement to

Center/forward Jerry Lucas, 32, dribbles past Wilt Chamberlain of the Los Angeles Lakers. Lucas helped the Knicks reach the NBA Finals in two of his three seasons with the team.

stop the Celtics' Jo Jo White. Meminger played the entire second quarter, scoring nine points to White's two. The Knicks rallied to take a 45–40 halftime lead. They then outscored the Celtics 37–22 to start the second half. New York won the game 94–78.

The Knicks would face the Lakers again in the Finals. To claim the championship, New York would have to become the first NBA team to beat two 60-win teams in the postseason. The Knicks lost the series opener. But they then won four straight to win the championship. As usual, they did it by sharing the ball. Bill Bradley led the way in Game 2 with 26 points. Monroe paced the team with 21 in Game 3, DeBusschere scored 33 in

Game 4, and Monroe had 23 in Game 5. Reed again was named the Finals MVP.

"We were not the biggest or the fastest," Frazier recalled. "But we were the smartest. And we were the best." Added Lucas: "I loved playing with that group of players. It was the way basketball should be played. I think that Knicks team—and I stress the word team—may have been the greatest team ever assembled."

But one thing teamwork could not conquer was age. New York reached the Eastern Conference finals the next year, but they lost in five games to the Celtics. Reed, DeBusschere, and Lucas all retired after that season. New York would win only one more playoff series the rest of the decade. The team tried reviving its fortunes by adding

VIBRANT VOICES

The Knicks have had legendary broadcasters.

Marty Glickman, an Olympic-caliber sprinter who was their first radio voice, helped listeners understand the geography of the court by inventing expressions such as "the key," "the lane," "the top of the circle," and "the midcourt stripe." He described baskets as "Good . . . like Nedick's!" (a hot-dog chain that sponsored games) or with an emphatic "Swish!" That was a term he borrowed from early Knicks players like Sonny Hertzberg and Leo Gottlieb when he shot baskets with them. Glickman was the radio voice of the Knicks from the 1940s to the 1960s.

Play-by-play man Marv Albert, a former ballboy, called Knicks games from 1967 to 1997, and again from 1998 to 2004. Albert was famous for his "Yes!" call, and for saying a dunk was made "with authority!"

established stars such as forward/centers Spencer Haywood and Bob McAdoo, and by naming Reed coach, but little worked.

Red Holzman had stepped down after the 1976–77 season. He returned as coach early in the 1978–79 campaign and went on to lead the Knicks to a 50-win season in 1980–81 behind young guards Ray Williams and Micheal Ray Richardson. But the legendary leader retired again after the 1981–82 season when the team slipped to 33–49. Holzman's replacement, Hubie Brown, turned over most of the roster and found a spark in forward Bernard King. King was a native New Yorker who was acquired in a trade that October.

An explosive scorer, King led the Knicks to the playoffs in 1982–83. He repeated the feat in 1983–84. King averaged a club-record 26.3 points per game in the 1983–84 regular season. This included back-to-back 50-point games in road wins over the San Antonio Spurs and the Dallas Mavericks. He then put on a show in the playoffs. In the first round, New York defeated the Detroit Pistons in a best-of-five series. King scored 36, 46, 46, 41, and 44 points in the five games. In the last game, he willed the team to victory despite playing with two dislocated fingers and the flu. The Knicks lost the next series to the Celtics in seven games despite two more 40-point efforts by King.

The next season, King raised his game even higher. He had a team-record 60-point game against the New Jersey Nets. And he was averaging 32.9 points per game after 55 games. But then his right knee buckled as he tried to block a

High-scoring Bernard King (30) joined the Knicks in 1982 and helped them reach the playoffs in the 1982–83 and 1983–84 seasons.

shot. "My knee just shattered," he said. "I just felt the most excruciating pain I ever felt in my life." King collapsed to the floor with a torn ligament. He would never be the same. King missed the entire next season and was released after playing just six games in 1986–87.

After the stirring performance in the 1983–84 playoffs, the Knicks were beset by injuries to King and others. New York did not win more than 24 games in any of the next three seasons.

King of the Court

"He's like a bird. He's swooping toward the basket and you think he's descending. Then, all of a sudden, at the last instant, he elevates and you'll see an incredible move." —Knicks coach Hubie Brown, on forward Bernard King

CHAPTER 4

THE EWING ERA

Dave DeBusschere, a star forward from the Knicks' championship era, was New York's general manager in May 1985. That month, the once-proud franchise joined with the six other non-playoff teams to participate in the NBA's first lottery. The drawing would determine the selection order for the draft of college players.

The grand prize was the right to pick first and choose Patrick Ewing. He was a skyscraper of a center who had starred for Georgetown University. The blind draw came down to two teams, the Indiana Pacers and the New York Knicks. As commissioner David Stern prepared to announce the runner-up team, DeBusschere wiped his brow.

"I'd rather be taking the last shot in a championship game than waiting for a card to be opened," he recalled.

Patrick Ewing blocks a shot against the Chicago Bulls in Game 7 of the Eastern Conference semifinals at Madison Square Garden in May 1994.

THE BIG MAN

"He has a heart of a champion," Chicago Bulls superstar Michael Jordan said about Knicks center Patrick Ewing. "He came and gave life back into the city."

Ewing never won an NBA title, in large part because Jordan blocked his way. But he was an 11-time All-Star and an intimidating low-post presence who made New York a perennial contender. The 7-foot big man joined the Knicks in 1985 from Georgetown University and averaged 21 points and 9.8 rebounds per game for his career. He is the team's all-time leader in points, rebounds, blocked shots, and steals. He averaged 20 points per game or more in each of his first 13 seasons.

"His unselfishness, leadership, passion, loyalty—that's what it was all about," said Jeff Van Gundy, New York's coach from 1996 to 2001. "He's definitely the best Knick ever."

What DeBusschere heard next was as pretty as a ball slicing through the net. Stern unsealed an envelope containing the Pacers' logo and announced that Indiana would pick second. That meant the Knicks had found a path back to prominence.

"We've had the [George] Mikan era, the [Bill] Russell era, the Kareem [Abdul-Jabbar] era . . . now we'll have the Ewing era," CBS sportscaster Pat O'Brien said, quoting an unnamed NBA scouting director.

Ewing lived up to the hype and was named NBA Rookie of the Year for the 1985–86 season. The Knicks began putting key pieces around him. They hired coach Rick Pitino and drafted point guard Mark Jackson. New York started poorly in 1987–88. But they used an all-out defensive style

From left, Kiki Vandeweghe, Patrick Ewing, and Mark Jackson share a laugh with Knicks coach Rick Pitino during the final minutes of a game in the 1989 Eastern Conference semifinals.

to win 22 of their final 37 games. The team made the playoffs for the first time since 1984.

New York would not miss the postseason for the next 14 seasons. The Knicks improved by 14 games to a record of 52–30 in 1988–89. The team made a then-NBA-season-record 386 three-point field goals to win the Atlantic Division for the first time since 1970–71. But Pitino left that summer for a college job. The Knicks slipped to 45 and 39 wins the next two seasons.

To reach the next level, New York needed a visionary leader. Enter Pat Riley. He was named coach in May 1991.

Knicks center Patrick Ewing pumps up the Madison Square Garden fans during Game 7 of the Eastern Conference semifinals against the Chicago Bulls in May 1994.

Riley had led the Los Angeles Lakers to four championships in the 1980s. His goal was to make the Knicks the "the best-conditioned, hardest-working, most-professional, unselfish, toughest, nastiest, and most-disliked team in the NBA."

Riley was demanding, and he got results. The Knicks won 51 games in his first season. They reached the Eastern Conference semifinals before losing in seven games to the eventual champion Chicago Bulls. In his second season, New York won 60 games, tying a club record. The Knicks advanced to the conference finals before once again losing to the Bulls.

In Riley's third season, 1993–94, the Knicks broke through to the NBA Finals. They beat the New Jersey Nets in the first round. They then ended the Bulls' three-year title run in the second round. Chicago was without recently-retired superstar Michael Jordan.

In the Eastern Conference finals, New York met Indiana. The Pacers took a three-games-to-two lead at Madison Square Garden behind 25 fourth-quarter points by Reggie Miller. But the Knicks evened the series on the road with a 98–91 victory. John Starks's 26 points and Derek Harper's late jumper and steal sparked the win.

New York trailed Game 7 at home by a point when Ewing rebounded a missed layup by Starks and slammed the ball through the hoop with both hands with 26.9 seconds left. New York prevailed 94–90.

Ewing finished with 24 points, 22 rebounds, and seven assists. He celebrated by leaping onto a table on press row.

The victory landed the Knicks in the NBA Finals for the first time since 1972–73. They would face the Houston Rockets and come tantalizingly close to winning it all. One night after the New York Rangers won the National Hockey League's Stanley Cup,

Sparks from Starks

Signed in 1988 out of the minor leagues, 6-foot-5 shooting guard John Starks was driven to prove himself. He played with fire and emotion. "Sometimes I can control it, and sometimes I just let it overflow," he said. Whether head-butting the Pacers' Reggie Miller, tomahawk-slamming over the Bulls' Horace Grant and Michael Jordan, or nearly propelling the Knicks to the 1994 NBA title in Game 6 of the Finals, Starks was a fan favorite. He is New York's all-time leader in three-pointers made.

the Knicks made their own bid for glory. New York won the fourth game 91–82 to tie the series at two games apiece. The Knicks won the fifth game 91–84. They then went to Houston seeking to clinch. It almost happened. Starks rallied the Knicks with 15 points in the final 9 minutes and 11 seconds. With New York down by two, Starks had a chance to win the game and the title with a last-second three-pointer. "It was money," Starks recalled of his shot. But Rockets center Hakeem Olajuwon leaped and barely deflected it off course.

Starks's touch eluded him in Game 7. The guard had shot 5-for-7 in the fourth quarter in Game 6. But he went just 2-for-18 from the field in the finale, including 0-for-11 from three-point range. The Knicks lost 90–84.

Riley didn't blame Starks. "John almost single-handedly the other night won it for us in Game 6," Riley said. "But you go with your players. You win with them and you lose with them. He's one of the greatest competitors I've ever met."

The loss was devastating because as of 2011 the Knicks have not since gotten quite that close.

In the Eastern Conference semifinals the next year,

Coach Pat Riley brought the Knicks to the NBA Finals during the 1993–94 season. His Knicks teams went to the playoffs in each of his four seasons.

New York again faced the Pacers. Miller stole Game 1 at the Garden. He scored eight points, including two three-pointers, in the final 16 seconds. Indiana took a three-games-to-one lead before Ewing, playing with a sore calf, won Game 5 with a runner in the final seconds. He then scored 25 points in a Game 6 victory. In Game 7, Ewing scored 29 points. But he missed a finger roll at the buzzer that ended the Knicks' season. One month later, an era ended as Riley resigned as coach.

"I just hope that whatever is thought of me and my four years there, it's that I came there to change things, and I did," Riley said. "We turned things around, and the Knicks became respected again in the NBA."

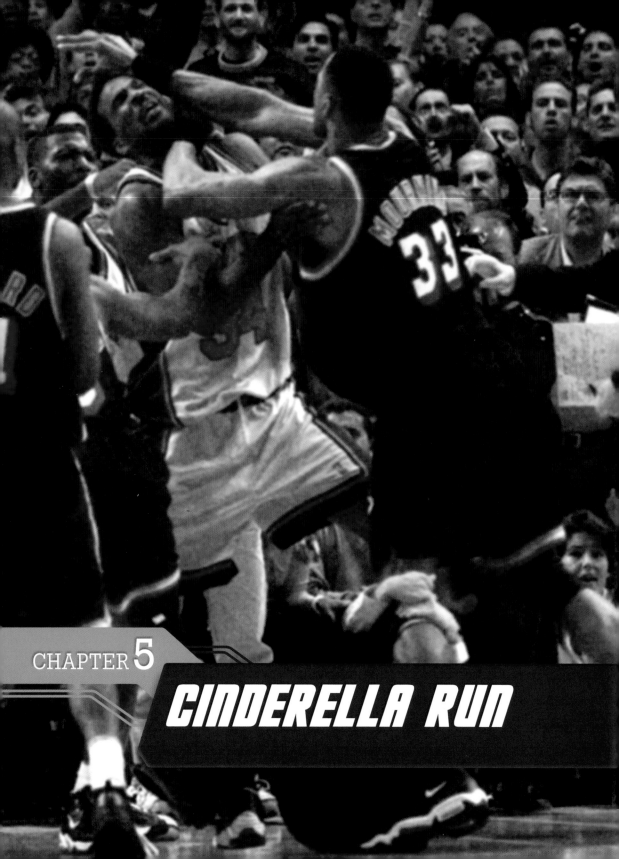

CHAPTER 5

CINDERELLA RUN

To move forward in 1995–96, the Knicks hired three-time NBA Coach of the Year Don Nelson. Nelson's loose practices, easy manner, and up-tempo offense were much different from life with Pat Riley.

But when the Knicks lost nine of 13 games in early March, Nelson was fired. The team replaced him with assistant coach Jeff Van Gundy. New York dropped its first game under Van Gundy. The Knicks then hosted Michael Jordan, who had come out of retirement, and the Chicago Bulls. The Bulls arrived at the Garden with a 54–6 record. New York trailed 56–54 early in the third quarter, but then outscored Chicago 50–16. The Knicks held the Bulls 34 points under their season scoring average, and the 104–72 victory opened eyes. "I couldn't believe it," Bulls guard Steve Kerr said. "They looked just like they did in the Pat Riley days."

The Miami Heat's Alonzo Mourning, *right*, and the Knicks' Charles Oakley fight in the first round of the 1998 Eastern Conference playoffs as Knicks coach Jeff Van Gundy holds onto Mourning's left leg.

The new Knicks looked like the Knicks of old. Van Gundy's pressure defense and grind-it-out offense suited the team's feisty personality. New York finished in second place in the Atlantic Division. The Knicks advanced to the Eastern Conference semifinals but lost to the Bulls, the NBA's eventual champions.

The next season, the Knicks led the Miami Heat, coached by Riley, three games to one in the conference semifinals. But New York lost five players to suspensions after a fight during Game 5. Miami rallied to win the series. In 1997–98, the same teams met in the first round of the postseason and battled again—Van Gundy clung to Heat center Alonzo Mourning's leg to break up a Game 4 fight with Knicks forward Larry Johnson. The Knicks evened the series at two games apiece. New York then won the decisive Game 5, advancing to the next round. But the Knicks lost for a third straight year in the conference semifinals. This time they fell to the Indiana Pacers.

To find a way over the hump, New York's front office had a busy off-season. The Knicks traded for Marcus Camby over the summer. He

All-Star guard Latrell Sprewell helped the Knicks advance to the 1999 NBA Finals.

was the league's leading shot-blocker. The team then added three-time All-Star guard Latrell Sprewell and power forward Kurt Thomas right before the February season opener—the 1998–99 season was shortened three months because of a dispute between NBA owners and players. The Knicks barely made the play-offs. They needed wins in six of their final eight games to

World's Most Famous Arena

The current Madison Square Garden, the fourth version of the Garden, is the second-oldest arena in the NBA. The arena has hosted thousands of events, including a heavyweight title bout between boxers Muhammad Ali and Joe Frazier, a visit from Pope John Paul II, and the Concert for New York after the 9/11 terrorist attacks. "There are bigger venues and newer venues," Knicks legend Walt Frazier said, "but there is only one Madison Square Garden. It is still 'the place.'"

The Knicks' Chris Childs (1), Allan Houston (20), and Marcus Camby (23) celebrate after their 72–70 victory in Game 6 of the 2000 Eastern Conference semifinals against Miami.

finish 27–23 and earn the East's eighth and final berth.

But "once we got in, anything could happen," Sprewell said. "And that's exactly what happened."

In the first round, the Knicks again played the Heat. Like the previous two seasons against Miami, the series came down to a winner-take-all game.

The Heat led the finale by one point. But Knicks guard Allan Houston took a 14-foot runner that bounced off the rim, kissed the backboard, and dropped through the net with 0.8 of a second remaining. New York survived 78–77 and became only the second eighth-seeded team in playoff history to defeat a number one seed.

New York then scorched the Atlanta Hawks for its first four-game playoff sweep since 1969. This put the Knicks in the conference finals against the Pacers. After the teams split in Indiana, the Knicks trailed 91–88 with 5.7 seconds left in Game 3. Johnson launched a three-point prayer from the wing. Not only did the desperation shot go in, but the forward also was fouled on the play and made his free throw for an unlikely 92–91 victory.

The Pacers evened the series in Game 4. But visiting New York won Game 5 behind 29 points from Sprewell. The Knicks then clinched the series 90–82 in Game 6 at Madison Square Garden. Houston scored 32 points in the finale as New York held its nemesis, Reggie Miller, to 3-for-18 from the field. When the final horn sounded, Knicks guard Chris Childs flung the ball into the stands. Van Gundy, whose job had been in jeopardy, ran downcourt and jumped into Houston's arms.

After the game, Knicks president Dave Checketts said, "I think it's one of the great stories in the history of the franchise."

It was also one of the last great stories in the history of the franchise. An injured Ewing was not available to play in the 1999 Finals against the San Antonio Spurs. So New York lacked the size to compete against the twin towers of David Robinson and Tim Duncan. The Spurs won the championship series four games to one.

The Knicks had one more run left in them. In 1999–2000, they swept an opening-round series against the Toronto Raptors. New York then eliminated the Heat on Miami's home floor for the third straight season, winning the seventh game 83–82 on Ewing's dunk with a minute and 20 seconds remaining. But New York ran out of magic in the Eastern Conference finals, losing to Indiana in six games.

Ewing, then 38 years old, was traded before the next season. Through the 2009–10 season, the Knicks had played in only two playoff series since. They lost to the Raptors three games to two in 2001, and to the New Jersey Nets four games to none in 2004. Through the rest of the decade, the closest New York came to a winning record was 16 games under .500.

The Knicks' outlook began to brighten in May 2008. That month, the team hired coach Mike D'Antoni away from the Phoenix Suns. Two years later, he lured one of his former stars, Amar'e Stoudemire, to the Big Apple. Stoudemire received a five-year contract. At the news conference held to announce the deal, the power forward energized the fan base, which was eager to relive the excitement that Willis Reed, Walt Frazier, and Patrick Ewing had brought to New York.

Stoudemire did it by saying four words: "The Knicks are back."

The Knicks ended the 2010–11 season with three superstars on their roster. They are, *from left*, Carmelo Anthony, Amar'e Stoudemire, and Chauncey Billups.

The Knicks, however, were not finished with their attempt to march back into the playoffs. On February 22, 2011, the Knicks pulled off an incredible trade in which they obtained 26-year-old Carmelo Anthony and 34-year-old Chauncey Billups from the Denver Nuggets.

The Knicks found success again in 2011. They finished with a 42–40 record and made the playoffs for the first time in seven seasons.

The Knicks were swept in the first round by Boston. But with Anthony, Stoudemire, and Billups, the team once again had hope for the future.

TIMELINE

1946 — The Knicks defeat the host Toronto Huskies 68–66 on November 1 in the first game in the BAA. The league would later merge with the NBL to form the NBA. Leo Gottlieb leads New York with 12 points.

1951 — The Knicks advance to the second-ever NBA Finals and face the Rochester Royals in an all–New York state title round.

1953 — New York advances to the NBA Finals for a third consecutive year, but again falls to the Minneapolis Lakers, this time in five games.

1967 — Two years after he was drafted, forward Bill Bradley makes his Knicks debut on December 9 before a rare Garden sellout. He scores eight points in 20 minutes, but New York falls 124–121 to the Detroit Pistons.

1970 — Walt Frazier's 36 points and 19 assists in Game 7 of the Finals against the Los Angeles Lakers on May 8 help the host Knicks win 113–99 for their first NBA championship.

1972 — The Knicks reach the NBA Finals but fall in five games to the Lakers.

1973 — Rallying from a 17-point second-half deficit on April 22, the Knicks beat the visiting Boston Celtics 117–110 in double overtime to take a three-games-to-one series lead in the Eastern Conference finals.

1984 — Forward Bernard King has 50-point games at San Antonio and Dallas on January 31 and February 1, respectively. The next season, he scores a franchise-record 60 at home against the New Jersey Nets on December 25.

1985	In the NBA's first draft lottery on May 12, the Knicks win the right to select first. On June 18, they pick Georgetown University center Patrick Ewing.
1990	The Knicks end a 26-game losing streak at Boston Garden on May 6 with a 121–114 victory over the Celtics in Game 5 of their first-round playoff series. New York also becomes the third team in NBA history to rally from a two-games-to-none deficit to win a best-of-five series.
1993	On February 4, the Knicks begin a nine-year, 433-game home sellout streak.
1994	Ewing's two-handed slam off John Starks's missed layup with 26.9 seconds left lifts New York to a 94–90 win over the Indiana Pacers in Game 7 of the Eastern Conference finals on June 5. The Knicks would go on to fall in seven games to the Houston Rockets in the NBA Finals.
1999	The Knicks become the first eighth seed to win a conference title, defeating the visiting Pacers 90–82 in Game 6 of the Eastern finals on June 11. New York would then lose in five games to the San Antonio Spurs in the NBA Finals.
2010	The Knicks acquire power forward Amar'e Stoudemire from the Phoenix Suns on July 9. Stoudemire goes on to have an All-Star season in 2010–11, ranking among the league's top scorers.
2011	Four-time All-Star forward Carmelo Anthony and five-time All-Star guard Chauncey Billups join the Knicks as part of a three-team trade on February 22.

43

QUICK STATS

FRANCHISE HISTORY
New York Knicks (1946–)

NBA FINALS
(1950– ; wins in bold)

1951, 1952, 1953, **1970**, 1972, **1973**, 1994, 1999

BAA FINALS

(1947–49)
None

KEY PLAYERS
(position[s]; years with team)

Carmelo Anthony (F; 2011–)
Dick Barnett (G; 1965–73)
Bill Bradley (F/G; 1967–77)
Carl Braun (G/F; 1947–61)

Dave DeBusschere (F; 1968–74)
Patrick Ewing (C; 1985–2000)
Walt Frazier (G; 1967–77)
Harry Gallatin (F/C; 1948–57)
Richie Guerin (G; 1956–63)
Allan Houston (G; 1996–2005)
Bernard King (F; 1982–1987)
Bob McAdoo (C/F; 1976–79)
Earl Monroe (G; 1971–80)
Charles Oakley (F; 1988–98)
Willis Reed (C/F; 1964–74)
John Starks (G; 1990–98)
Amar'e Stoudemire (C/P; 2010–)

KEY COACHES

Red Holzman (1967–77, 1978–82):
    613–484; 54–43 (postseason)
Joe Lapchick (1947–56):
    326–247; 30–30 (postseason)
Pat Riley (1991–95):
    223–105; 35–28 (postseason)

HOME ARENAS

69th Regiment Armory (1946–60)
Madison Square Garden (old)
    (1946–68)
Madison Square Garden (new)
    (1968–)

*All statistics through 2010–11 season

QUOTES AND ANECDOTES

The Knicks had the NBA's first Asian player, guard Wataru Misaka of Japan, in 1947, and one of the league's first three African Americans, center Nat "Sweetwater" Clifton, in 1950. Misaka, at 5 feet 7, was the shortest Knick ever. Clifton got his nickname because he loved soda pop.

Hall of Fame center/forward Jerry Lucas memorized the first 500 pages of the Manhattan phone directory. Lucas, a Knick from 1971 to 1974, was also known for his memory while playing for Ohio State University. *Sports Illustrated* reported that he would spell a word aloud, but then rearrange the word's letters alphabetically. "Thus, basketball becomes aabbekllst."

All nine of the Knicks' NBA Finals home games in 1951, 1952, and 1953 had to be played at the 69th Regiment Armory because Madison Square Garden was being used for the circus.

Guard Dick "Fall Back Baby" Barnett was famous for the way he curled his body into a question mark and kicked back when taking jump shots.

"When you go to the mountaintop together, you are brothers for life. The bond is permanent." —Knicks Hall of Fame forward Bill Bradley, on his relationship with teammates with whom he won two NBA championships

In 2011, the Knicks overtook the Los Angeles Lakers as the NBA's most valuable franchise, according to *Forbes* magazine. The Knicks were valued at $655 million.

GLOSSARY

broadcaster

An announcer who describes or talks about sporting events on television or radio.

contract

A binding agreement about, for example, years of commitment by a basketball player in exchange for a given salary.

draft

A system used by professional sports leagues to select new players in order to spread incoming talent among all teams. The NBA Draft is held each June.

franchise

An entire sports organization, including the players, coaches, and staff.

general manager

The executive who is in charge of the team's overall operation. He or she hires and fires coaches, drafts players, and signs free agents.

intimidating

Putting fear into opponents.

overtime

A period in a basketball game that is played to determine a winner when the four quarters end in a tie.

perennial

Happening every year.

postseason

The games in which the best teams play after the regular-season schedule has been completed.

rebound

To secure the basketball after a missed shot.

resign

To give up a job or position.

veteran

An individual with great experience in a particular endeavor.

FOR MORE INFORMATION

Further Reading

Ballard, Chris. *The Art of a Beautiful Game: The Thinking Fan's Tour of the NBA*. New York: Simon & Schuster, 2009.

D'Agostino, Dennis. *Garden Glory: An Oral History of the New York Knicks*. Chicago: Triumph Books, 2003.

Gutman, Bill. *Tales from the 1969–1970 New York Knicks*. Champaign, IL: Sports Publishing LLC, 2005.

Web Links

To learn more about the New York Knicks, visit ABDO Publishing Company online at **www.abdopublishing.com**. Web sites about the Knicks are featured on our Book Links page. These links are routinely monitored and updated to provide the most current information available.

Places to Visit

Madison Square Garden
Two Pennsylvania Plaza
New York, NY 10121
212-465-6471
www.thegarden.com
This has been the Knicks' home arena since February 1968. The team plays 41 regular-season games here each year.

Naismith Memorial Basketball Hall of Fame
1000 West Columbus Avenue
Springfield, MA 01105
413-781-6500
www.hoophall.com
This hall of fame and museum highlights the greatest players and moments in the history of basketball. Walt Frazier and Willis Reed are among the former Knicks enshrined here.

The 69th Regiment Armory
68 Lexington Avenue
Regimental Headquarters
New York, NY 10010
646-424-5500
www.sixtyninth.net/armory.html
The armory, built in 1906, was the Knicks' second home from 1946 to 1960. Nine NBA Finals games were played there in 1951, 1952, and 1953.

INDEX

About the Author

Andy Knobel has worked at the *Baltimore Sun* since 1988, most recently as the Deputy Sports Editor for Nights. He previously worked for the *York* (Pa.) *Daily Record*, the *Post-Standard* in Syracuse, New York, and the *Cornell Daily Sun*. He was raised in New York City during the Knicks' championship years. He lives in Columbia, Maryland, with his wife and two children and has helped coach youth baseball, basketball, and soccer.